FROM GOOD T

For Erika
with love,
Michael

FROM GOOD

*No Bullshit Tips for
The Life You Always Wanted*

TO AMAZING

MICHAEL SERWA

RETHINK PRESS

First published in 2013 by Rethink Press
(www.rethinkpress.com)

To my parents.

Your enormous faith in me through all the ups and downs has been, and still is, extraordinary.

To my incredible friends and clients.

You are my inspiration, the reason why I get out of bed every morning.

PRAISE

"I rarely endorse any self help books. However, *From Good To Amazing* is an exceptional book, which underlines what is truly important in life in a simple and easy way whilst being profoundly thought provoking. Michael Serwa has a unique gift to be able to wade through complexities of modern life with a clear and directive approach. You can spot many glimpses of authenticity and Michael's dedication to truly serve those who cross his path through this wonderful book."

Darshana Ubl - CEO, Entrevo UK | KPI Programme, Serial Entrepreneur

"I like this book and I like Michael Serwa. This book is written for successful people who want to become more successful. It's not a lesson, it's a reminder! The fast chapters serve to tune you into your best self. Even as I skimmed through the first time, I felt my energy rising. It's the kind of book you want to have on your iPhone as a daily dose of motivation."

Daniel Priestley - Entrepreneur and Author

"This book removes *all* excuses. If you read it from start to finish, you have absolutely no reason not to be extraordinary. Michael's style is brilliant. Cutting the BS, to the point and totally focused on creating action."

Jean-Pierre De Villiers - Celebrity Trainer and Founder of Reshape Life

"Outrageously inspiring, wise and actionable. Michael has packed this book with ideas that will shake up and wake up every aspect of your life."

Jacqueline Biggs - International best-selling author of 'Marketing to Win', JacquelineBiggs.com

"If there was one book that, with its simple-to-follow steps, helps you kick start your journey to not only clean up your life, but also to create an amazing life, it's this one. I started to read it and it's one of these books you read in one day: you don't fall asleep reading it; you don't put it down until you have read it; and for sure you want to keep it in your collection of inspirational books you reach for each time the self doubt kicks in. No matter where you might be in your journey of life, you will find something here that will open your eyes to see the amazing you. I feel I've just found a book I can recommend to everyone I know. Thank you for creating this fantastic manual for life."

Tony Jeton Selimi - Founder of The Velvet Journey and HealOneSelf

"The contents list alone is a comprehensive kick up the butt. I like the quirkiness and directness of the bite-sized chapters, too."

Ben Harrington - Education Ambassador at Peace One Day

"You know the old saying, 'Only rocket science is rocket science and this isn't rocket science'? Well, it is applicable to Michael's book! Why? Because the book will not offer you complicated ideas or fancy stuff, but what it does offer you is the opportunity to constantly remind yourself of the concepts that you must execute on a daily basis. I guess you could call this the daily fuel to your rocket. Without fuel it doesn't matter how amazing your rocket is because it will simply not fly!"

Vineet Bhatia - Founder of Guru Coach

CONTENTS

INTRODUCTION

I believe our ultimate purpose in life is happiness. I believe that unless we're happy nothing else really matters. Happiness will mean different things to different people, but the bottom line is that whatever we do, whether we try to avoid pain or gain pleasure, it's all about happiness.

I've dedicated my life to helping people identify and achieve their goals, find balance, and therefore increase their happiness. My mission is to assist them in becoming the best they can possibly be, one person or one group of people at the time.

What I also believe is that the process of transforming our lives, or certain areas of our lives, doesn't need to take years. I've helped hundreds of amazing men and women to become better versions of themselves within months or even weeks.

Can you transform your life just by reading this book? Technically you can; realistically you probably won't. I share here with you some of my top ideas from different areas of personal development. I have put them in a random order so you can read, and implement them in any order you like. They are, though, just ideas – and not even original ones, as pretty much everything about personal development was said in the 20th century. It is the implementation of these ideas that is the hard part. Unless you're very disciplined and motivated, get yourself the best coach, mentor or personal trainer you can afford to assist you, to be in your corner. It will be the best money you've ever spent.

SET GOALS

Goals are dreams with deadlines. Setting goals is the single most important exercise you can do for your own self-development. If you are serious about your growth, you have to have goals. Personal goals, professional goals, financial goals, fitness goals, all sorts of goals.

Speaking of fitness goals, I remember one of my clients writing his very first goal: 'I want to look good naked.' It made me laugh. 'I'm sure your girlfriend will fully support you on this one,' I said. I was particularly motivated in helping him to achieve this goal as she was the one who had found me to help him. I thought I owed her at least that much.

Having no goals is like being on a boat without a sail. The wind of life will blow, but you will find yourself drifting. We can't control all life's circumstances and events, but what we can control is the cut of the sail and how we catch the wind and use it to push us where we want to go. The risk we take is that unless we know where we're heading we might end up somewhere we don't want to be.

There are four elements of goal setting: What, By when, Why and How.

First, ask yourself what it is that you want, and just write it down. You can break your goals down into separate areas or just write one long list. Aim for minimum of 10 to start with; it shouldn't take you more than 10 minutes. If you think you don't know 10 things that you want, trust me, you do. Just start writing: short-term goals and long-term goals, things you can do tomorrow and things that may take you years to accomplish.

Second, next to each of them, write a deadline. It can be one day, two weeks, five years, or January

2020, for example, whichever way you prefer for each goal.

Third, ask yourself why you want what you want. Write a minimum of three reasons why you want to achieve each goal.

I remember running a goal-setting workshop and one young woman's goal was to get married. As soon as she started to write her 'whys' she realised it wasn't actually her goal and she crossed it out. The first 'why' was, 'because my mum wants me to get married'; the second, 'because my dad wants me to get married'.

If you don't really understand why you're doing what you're doing, you're going to seriously struggle in sticking to your actions. Good reasons why will allow your motivation to reach the emotional part of your brain, which will result in you acting consistently to achieve change.

sure what you want is the product of your own conclusions.

Fourth, think about and write down all the actions you could take towards achieving your goal, both individual and repetitive ones. The more the better.

Every time you achieve a significant goal (or any goal, if you want), celebrate. As long as you don't celebrate finally quitting drinking by opening a bottle of champagne, everything is fine.

Review your goals regularly, at least once every three months. Remove those you've already achieved or are no longer relevant, and add some new ones if needed. Make sure the list is always full.

Some of the people involved in NASA's 1969 first moon expedition experienced* serious psychological breakdowns after the expedition was completed. Why? They spent years in preparation for that one mission and after it was over they found themselves with nothing to look forward to, with no other goals. NASA learnt from that experience to make sure that people involved in the second expedition had some other, external goals throughout the process.

Make sure at least some of your goals are big. If our goals don't scare us it means they're not big enough. I have to tell you, some of my goals scare the crap out of me, so I know I'm good for now.

One of the greatest lessons I've learnt about achieving goals is from my teacher, Jim Rohn (check him out on YouTube if you don't know him; the best speaker I've ever seen). Jim says it's not what we get in life, it's who we become. The most valuable outcome from attracting the great partner we always wanted for example, is not that partner; it's the kind of person we had to become to attract them in the first place.

STOP TALKING, START DOING

Talking is easy. The problem is, just talking is a waste of time. It's all about taking action. You can think and talk, and then think some more, but if you don't do anything with it, it's all for nothing. You can spend years contemplating certain ideas, but ideas are cheap – every guy and his dog has an idea, it's all about their implementation. At the end of the day, you won't produce anything by contemplation alone. Only those who actually produce are the ones that move forward.

Don't expect to necessarily enjoy the whole process of getting where you want to get to, either. Mohammed Ali said that he hated training, but he figured he would suffer now to live the rest of his life as a champion. I don't like to write, but I love the idea that what I'm writing might make a difference in your life. I love the idea that, thanks to this book, you and I might meet one day and work together on taking your life to the next level. So I had a choice: contemplating the idea of writing this book or just sitting down and getting on with it.

My favourite definition of success is that it comes from a few simple disciplines practised every day. Note, it says *every* day, not every other day, not when it's nice weather or when we are in a good mood – '*every* day'. It's not rocket science: success can be achieved by a simple repeated action. What are you going to do today?

OVERCOME PROCRASTINATION

I call procrastination one of the biggest 'social diseases'. I see so many great, talented people screwing their chances of becoming the best they can be because of that 'disease'. I see them every day. Most of my clients, when they come to me for the first time, seriously procrastinate. It can be painful to watch.

Why do we procrastinate? The list of possible reasons is long and you will often find there is more than one in any given case. Fear is a big one. Fear of failure, fear of success, fear of change, fear of the unknown. Sometimes our desire just isn't strong enough. Sometimes our dreams or goals don't inspire us. Sometimes we lose the momentum or motivation. Negative self-talk and beliefs, being overwhelmed with too many options, having too many distractions that cause us to lose focus, avoiding discomfort, perfectionism... the list goes on and on. These are all both valid and common reasons for procrastinating.

Do you know what I find to be the biggest reason of all? You're not going to like hearing it, I'm warning you. Laziness. In my own life, my friends' lives and my clients' lives, that's the one I've seen the most. We don't like to hear it because who likes to think of themselves as lazy (it's so much more acceptable to think the reason for not doing something is a fear of failure, or being a perfectionist, for example)?

But here is the good news: being lazy about going to the gym, for example, doesn't make you a lazy person, it makes you a person who is lazy about going to the gym. I've never met anyone who is 100% lazy, or 100% free from laziness. We tend to be lazy about the things we don't like to do and ok doing the things we like. The problem comes when that thing we don't like doing is instrumental in moving forward with something important for us. I'm fortunate in that the thing I'm the laziest about is also one of the easiest to outsource – cleaning. And that my cleaning lady must be the best cleaning lady on the planet (I love her, I swear to God, if I ever move cities she's going with me).

You need to cut through the bullshit and correctly identify the reasons behind your procrastination so you can use the right strategy to overcome it. The best solution I know is accountability – one of the main reasons why coaching is so effective. Of course you can ask your partner, friend or colleague to hold you accountable, but it's not the same as having someone objective on your case once a week or 24/7, especially if you pay that person a lot of money for it. Not doing the things you commit to come with the sense of wasting that money.

Some other practical tips I want to give you are:

- get clear on your goals (make sure you understand why you're doing what you're doing)
- plan your day each day
- get rest when you're tired
- break down big, overwhelming tasks into smaller ones, and
- focus on starting rather than finishing.

A few years ago, before my cleaning lady came into my life, when I used to vacuum my flat myself, I realised that although I never looked forward to doing it, once I had started (here is the important bit) I never felt like stopping. Not only that, more often than not I would get into it to the point where I almost enjoyed it.

The point is, all we need to do is to start doing the thing we don't really feel like doing. We can trick our mind by saying that all we need to do is to spend a minute on it, no big deal, just one minute. Whether it's cleaning, running, job-searching or talking about where things are between you and your partner, nine times out of 10, after spending an initial minute you will keep doing what you have started. Ta-da! You have just tricked your procrastinating mind using the 'one-minute rule'. Try it tomorrow. Or even better – today!

DISCOVER YOUR VALUES

Knowing your core values is instrumental in achieving your goals.

Why?

You will seriously struggle to be happy if you go through life doing things that go against those values and, if you don't know them, you won't know what you working against. Take a minute to ask yourself, what are your three most important values?

Here are some examples: love, respect, fun, stability, integrity, adventure, financial success, recognition, freedom, authenticity, growth... the list is endless.

Let me illustrate. One of my values is fun. No matter what I do, and who I do it with, I have to have fun. I've designed my life in a way that I can experience a lot of it, and I'm not talking about going out kind of fun. My work is fun for me (even though I deal with a lot of challenging stuff), the people I surround myself with are fun, the physical activities I engage in are fun. My whole life is designed around it. Why? Because I know fun is one of my core values and misalignment with it would lead to unhappiness.

Bear in mind that our values may change over time, as we get older, wiser and more experienced. Hence we want to review them regularly, especially if a lot is going on in our lives. Sometimes one big event can turn things upside down. That's fine, be flexible. It's not about what your values are, it's about living in alignment with them, whatever they are.

BE THE WEIGHT YOU ARE HAPPY WITH

I find being underweight, and particularly overweight, is one of the biggest causes of unhappiness and confidence issues. We need two things to get our weight where we want it to be: some basic knowledge about how our body works; and discipline, a lot of discipline. I can't teach you discipline here, but I can certainly share with you a couple of facts that I always do with people before I put them on one of my weight loss/gain programmes.

1. We all have a built in 'thermostat', set on a certain weight and, no matter what we do and how we do it, that thermostat will always try to keep our weight on that level. If you are lucky, the weight yours is set on will be also the weight you are happy with. For the rest of us, it will always be a struggle.

I know my thermostat is set on around 72 kg (159 lbs), 13kg (22lbs) less than I am right now, which is the weight I'm happy with. I feel and look way too skinny when I'm on 72kg, considering my height. To stay on 85 kg, though, I have to constantly discipline myself to eat more than I feel like. The moment I stop paying attention, I'm losing weight, no matter how hard I push myself in the gym.

It's like an inner civil war between what our mind wants and what our body wants. Most of us lose the war to our body and end up with a weight we are not happy with. As I said, it takes lots of self-discipline, in my case to eat more than I want, for many of you eating less than you want.

2. Losing/gaining weight is around 75% about how much we eat and 25% about the exercise we do or don't do. Signing up for a gym (even a fancy one, believe it or not) won't change much (as far as losing / gaining weight is concerned, though it has plenty of other benefits) if we don't change our daily calorie intake.

The bottom line is this - if we want to lose weight, we have to eat less calories than we burn and if we want to gain weight, we have to eat more calories than we burn. There is no way around it.

Let's say you're an average male and you need 2,500 calories a day just to maintain your body weight. To lose a pound a week you need to decrease daily calorie intake by around 500 and to gain a pound you need to increase it by 500.

Running for half an hour will burn around 300 calories, the equivalent of a cheeseburger. Whether you run and have that cheeseburger (and we tend to be hungrier than usual after any exercise) or don't run and don't have it, as far as the calorie count is concerned you do exactly the same thing. Are you following me? It doesn't matter how much you exercise, if you don't eat fewer calories than you burn your body weight will never go down. On the other side, if you don't eat more calories than your body burns your weight will never go up.

CREATE YOUR OWN OPPORTUNITIES

We have two options: waiting for things to happen or making things happen; waiting for an opportunity to come or creating one. Waiting for a better economic climate, for somebody else to give us a break, waiting for 'when I'm ready'. The problem with waiting is that we might wait forever.

We are often only as far away from making a massive difference in our lives as making a phone call or visiting a website we wouldn't normally visit.

Some of us look at successful people – successful in any area – and say that they must have got lucky. I don't believe in luck. I believe we make our own luck. Seneca said, 'Luck is where the crossroads of opportunity and preparation meet.'

One of the things I found out about the Universe is that when we set an intention and start to act on it, the Universe, through other people or circumstances, co-operates with us. It will bring that thing you want two steps closer for every little step you take towards it.

Put yourself out there and discover infinite possibilities.

TAKE FULL RESPONSIBILITY

One of the biggest blocks I encounter in my coaching practice is when people don't want to take full responsibility for their current circumstances. I know that until they do so, I will struggle to help them. The blame list is long, starting from relatives and teachers, through the economy and government, to the weather!

I have bad news for you, I'm afraid. The only real problem you have is you: your limiting beliefs, lack of motivation and procrastination. On the flip side, though, it's good news because if it's you, you can do something about it, right?

Putting ourselves in the position of 'victim' makes us powerless. Taking responsibility, on the other hand, however uncomfortable it might feel, allows us to start the process of change.

Let's accept that we are not perfect, that we make mistakes and fail sometimes. But let's realise also that this is absolutely fine, as long as we don't try to shift the blame onto someone or something else and therefore prevent ourselves from moving forward.

DE-CLUTTER

I find that, as a general rule, the clutter in our surroundings is the reflection of our mental clutter. When I meet someone who is all over the place mentally, I can be almost certain their room or flat will be a mess.

First of all, de-clutter your mind. If you hate somebody, forgive them. If you hate yourself for doing or not doing something, forgive yourself. If you don't like something in your life, change it. If you can't change it, accept it. If you've been hurt in the past (welcome to the club), move on.

Think about negativity, blame, guilt, resentment as the mental equivalent of the clothes that you are never going to wear cluttering up your wardrobe. Get rid of both – you just don't need them.

Second of all, de-clutter your phone and computer, the two things that you probably use the most. Do you have 500 contacts on your phone, for instance, but only recognise half of them? Well, you can delete the rest as the chances that you will ever need to call someone whose name you don't recognise are rather slim, don't you think? On your computer, start with your inbox and clear up the backlog of emails, replying and/or deleting, and, after doing so, stay on top of it.

You can reply to over 90% of your emails within 48 hours if you commit to it. You've heard the saying that if you want to get something done you should ask a busy person to do it? The busiest people I know reply to me the fastest.

After clearing the backlog, move the remaining messages to appropriate folders; if you don't have folders, create them. Then go on and clear up the rest of your computer.

Third, go around your home and ask yourself whether you really, really need all the things you have. Perhaps you could give some stuff to charity. You don't need to end up looking like Steve Jobs, sitting on the floor of his furniture-less house, but there is certainly a lesson to be learnt there. Not so much from Jobs himself, but from Zen from where he took the idea for minimalistic decor.

De-cluttering your mind will inevitably lead to de-cluttering your surroundings, as you just won't be able to stand being in a messy environment when you feel happy, peaceful and clear about your both present and future. But it also works the other way around: tidying up the environment you're in will lead to feeling better and clearer about your future.

LET GO OF THE PAST

Past is past. I know, it is so great of me to enlighten you on that. Seriously, though, I know beyond a shadow of a doubt that one of the main reasons I've been in a good place mentally for a while is because I conditioned myself to not live in the past.

We want to be future focused. Not past focused. You can't focus on both so you had better choose wisely. The future of infinite possibilities, or the past with all the rejections you have experienced, all the mistakes you have made and all the things you wanted to do and didn't. Which approach do you think will make you a happier person?

We all have things in the past we wish were not there, but guess what, they are there and they will always be there. No amount of thinking and dwelling will change that, so why not acknowledge them, accept them and move on?

Move on to the question, what is it that I can do today to have the kind of future that I want to have? I can assure you that not one person who you consider to be great or highly successful got there by living in the past. Today is the first day of the rest of your life; what are you going to do about it?

WORK ON YOUR CONFIDENCE

Confidence is a big one. We need it to achieve just about anything, from something as tiny as leaving the house in the morning to asking someone out on a date.

We gain confidence by pushing ourselves across three zones. We all know the first one, our comfort zone. Some of us know it a little bit too well. Next there is a stretch zone and after that lies the panic zone. If we never go outside our comfort zone we will never grow our confidence (nor our character or bank account, by the way). The magic happens out there, beyond our comfort zone, when we stretch ourselves and experience a little discomfort as we do so. We can also jump from the first zone straight to the third one, but we don't have to. I personally like to use a graduated approach, for myself and people I work with, one step at a time, nice and relaxed. Well, as relaxed as stretching ourselves can be.

Confidence is a result of taking action. Practise it. Ask yourself in which areas you lack confidence the most; practise acting with confidence even if you don't feel it and, before you know it, things that were in your panic and stretch zones will be within your comfort zone.

TRY MEDITATION

I say 'try meditation' rather than 'meditate' because the fact that it is good for me and many people I know doesn't mean it will be good for you.

One of the biggest misconceptions about meditation is that it's a religious or spiritual practice. It certainly can be, and has been for centuries, but these days probably as many, if not more, non-religious as religious people regularly meditate. Mediation went mainstream in the 20th century.

I did a mediation course after having a sleeping disorder for six months. I didn't know it at the time, but it must have been something to do with the job I had and couldn't stand.

Before the course there was an initial consultation with one of the teachers in which she asked me why I had enrolled and what I wanted to get out of it. I told her about my issues with sleeping and she said to give it six weeks and it would be gone. 'Oh really?' I thought. Although I was sceptical, I went for it and started to meditate for 20 minutes, twice a day, every day. Within weeks I was sleeping like a baby and I've been sleeping like a baby ever since.

Improving quality of sleep is one out of the very many benefits of mediation. Try it if you would like to become calmer, more peaceful, more focused, more productive with any sort of work.

There are many techniques of meditation and every school will tell you that theirs is the best. What I will tell you is that they are all pretty much the same as far as possible benefits are concerned. 'Different technique' usually means a different object of meditation, such as breath, sound, candle flame, mantra (repeated word or combination of words). There is walking meditation, sitting meditation. You can meditate with your eyes closed or open, for five, 10, 30, 60 or more minutes at a time. I've personally tried several different approaches. The possibilities and variations are endless.

Pick the way that suits you best (you can learn it on one of many courses available, from a book or YouTube video) and try it every day for six weeks. Consistency is the key.

Over the years, I've recommended mediation to many people if I felt it could help them in one thing or another. Sometimes they have liked it and benefited from it; sometimes they haven't. If you won't try, you won't know.

QUIT COMPLAINING

People who know you well don't want to hear it; people who don't know you well don't want to hear it and really don't care.

Positive people are the most attractive, the easiest to be around. Being positive is not necessarily about having a big smile on your face 24/7 (I certainly don't), it's about not being negative to start with. Complaining plays such a big role in coming across as negative, doesn't it?

If we complain from time to time it's not a big deal, but if we do it all the time it means that it's a habit, and a very bad one. It makes biting your nails look innocent in comparison.

The good news about habits is that we can change them, and it's been said it can take as little as 21 days to do so. If you make a commitment to yourself not to complain at all for three weeks, the chances are that after this period complaining will not feel right for you anymore; it will feel unnatural.

STAY FIT

It's healthy, we all know that, but I'm not a doctor so I won't be elaborating on this aspect of staying fit. What I'm interested in is how being fit and engaging in the activities that allow us to stay fit affect our mental state, bringing us more happiness as well as energy and motivation to do things.

You're not going to wake up in the morning and think, 'I can conquer the world!' if you feel lousy. Our physiology has a huge impact on our state of mind and therefore any physical activity will improve our brain power and happiness levels. Our body releases all the good stuff (endorphins, serotonin, dopamine) when we exercise as well as for some time afterwards.

There are so many ways of staying fit. You should choose one, or more, that you enjoy because that's what you're most likely to stay committed to. I like heavy lifting, for example. You know the annoying guy in every gym making lots of noise? Well, I am that guy. But then you couldn't pay me enough to make me go for a run or do some other form of cardio. I just don't like it, it's not me. I take a lift to go one floor up, that's how much I dislike cardio. Before I reached this clear conclusion on what does and what doesn't do it for me, I tried just about everything. Try things; don't worry about what your partner or friends like to do, find out what you like to do, and do it.

Oh, and going round a golf course in a buggy doesn't count as physical activity, sorry. Sex does, though. That's like weight-lifting, cardio work and playing chess all at the same time.

HAVE MONEY

I like what Zig Ziglar said: 'Money isn't the most important thing in life, but it's reasonably close to oxygen on the (gotta have it) scale.' The way I look at money is that I want to have it so I don't need to think about getting it and I can fully focus on the things that are most important to me.

As long as you don't fool yourself that money alone will make you happy, you're good. When I was very young I thought that money alone does bring happiness; a typical way of thinking when you grow up in a family with little money and constantly worrying about it, I guess. Throughout my adult life I've had periods with a lot of money and then periods with no money at all. Looking back, I can't see my happiness levels being much affected by these different states.

People who win millions in the lottery, after an initial rise in happiness go back to the level they were at prior to winning after about a year. They are likely to end up feeling less happy because of all the new stress that comes with managing their money, investments and so on. I don't know about you, but I still wouldn't mind experiencing their pain.

Being poor in Western society just doesn't cut it. There is too much wealth around, constantly reminding us what we don't have if we're poor. Earn as much money as possible as fast as possible. Then go and share as much as you can with others to really appreciate its value.

LEARN TO BE
AMBITIOUS AND CONTENT

There are lots of ambitious people out there, and quite a few content ones as well. What's rare is to meet someone who is both ambitious and content. Wouldn't that be an ideal scenario? To have ambition pushing us to always reach for more but at the same time knowing how to appreciate who we are and what we have already. I love the way Jim Rohn put it: 'Be happy with what you have in the pursuit of what you want.'

GET RID OF TV

TV is one of the most costly things you can ever buy. It's not because of the price of the actual unit. It's because of all the money you could earn during the time you spend watching it.

Certain TV programs are great and you most definitely don't need to miss your favourite ones (I don't miss mine). The thing is, you can watch them online at a time set by you instead of watching them through the TV schedule and then inevitably watching things you don't care about that much just because they're there.

I sold my TV a few years ago and, considering I only got £20 for it, the word 'sold' looks like a serious overstatement. It was a 2005 Sony weighing 45kg (99 lbs). Nobody wanted it (I wonder why) and my concern was how on earth were we going to get this heavyweight piece of technology down the stairs. What were the chances of an ex-bodybuilder coming to buy it? I remember mentally high fiving the Universe after seeing the size of that guy when I opened the door for him.

If you're big on movies like I am, but you don't like to watch them on your laptop like I do, you could keep your TV just to watch them on a decent size screen.

STAY AWAY FROM NEGATIVE PEOPLE

There are three kinds of people: losers, winners and winners who need some coaching. The fact that you're reading this tells me that you're one of the two latter kinds.

We're the average of five people we spend the most time with. In terms of our happiness levels, fitness level, the size of our bank account, almost anything, we are likely to average those of the five people we spend the most time with. This is great if these five people are valuable (valuable will mean different things for each of us), but if you are spending most of your time with losers, they will bring you down because that's what they do (I like to think unconsciously) – they bring the rest of us down. If they don't believe they can do something themselves they will try to tell you that you can't do it either.

Other people have an enormous influence on us, whether we're aware of it or not. A great, supportive network of friends can make a massive difference in our lives. If your friends are not particularly supportive, find new ones! It's amazing how easy it is to make new good friends, unless you think it's difficult, that is, then in fact it will be.

Sometimes you need to let go of old, not so suitable anymore friends to make room for new ones. You don't need to eliminate them from your life completely because your values in life are different now, just limit the time you spend together. The moment you realise you get back nowhere near as much as you give to your friendship (support, value, attention, love) it's time to think whether it's the right friendship to have. Every minute spent with someone who is not contributing positively to our lives is potentially a minute not spent with someone who could. Now, I understand that this may sound difficult, especially if the negative people around you are family members, but for seven days observe how you feel when you limit your time spent with them to one day a week, how you feel on the other six days.

You may have to make family members an exception in what I'm talking about here. We don't choose them, but still, we can spend less time with those who we recognise as a bad influence on us. I like what Wayne Dyer said: 'Friends are God's way of apologising for your family'.

I have been fortunate to have some incredible friends throughout my life, but I'm not actively in touch with many of them anymore. Not because they stopped being great, but because our values, once the same, are different now, and that's ok!

My very best friend from my teens is one of the most interesting and successful theatre directors of my generation in Poland. We were best friends then because we shared a passion for art; for me it was mainly jazz and theatre and for him theatre and visual arts. The guy is a genius, but on the few occasions when we meet now we have very little to talk about. All he cares about is art and all I care about is personal development. Are we bothered? No, we both have new close friends, people we're on the same page with.

Some would argue that we can only trust people that we have known for years. I couldn't disagree more. It's not about the time, it's about the connection we make or don't make. There are some people I have spent literally a few hours with, who I feel I could rely on more than others I've known for years.

LOOK AT THE BIG PICTURE

Anything significant that was ever created started with a vision. Sometimes a vision is so huge it can be overwhelming; it can make the thing we want seem unattainable.

To work through to whatever we want to achieve we need to break the task down, into a first step, then a second... But because there will be difficulties along the way – there always are – we should never forget the big picture and never let 'little things cheat us out from the big opportunities', as Jim Rohn put it.

Write down the end goal, stick it somewhere you can see it every day or, even better, 10 times a day (I have mine on sticky notes on the wardrobe in front of my bed). Keep reminding yourself what the vision is as you deal with day-to-day hurdles.

REST

Rest well so you can do more and better by being more productive. Let's not confuse two words – activity and productivity. If you're tired you may still be active, but not necessarily productive.

When we don't get at least seven hours of sleep at night, we have low blood flow to the prefrontal cortex, the first third of our brain. This leads to reduced decision-making capacity. Of course, if you sleep a little less every now and then it's not a big deal as long as you don't make a habit of it.

A few years ago I discovered the power of naps. It still amazes me how a few minutes of sleep in the middle of the day can completely refresh my mind. I went all the way from 'I can't sleep during the day' to 'I can fall asleep pretty much anywhere within minutes'.

I visited a friend in Madrid some time ago. One day we called on a friend and planned to hit Madrid's nightlife scene afterwards. I was tired and asked this friend of my friend if I could use one of her beds for half an hour. After a few seconds of consternation, and realising that my plan didn't involve her, she showed me to one of her rooms. I had more energy that night than the whole bunch of my friends combined. The power of a nap is magical!

If you have never napped you may struggle to fall asleep the first couple of times. That's normal. Why? Because you've never done it before. Thoughts running through our head sometimes make it hard even if you're an experienced 'napper'. What I do (and I take 15-20-minute naps regularly on my 'gym days'), is listen to audio recordings to help me fall asleep. Focusing on anything (in my case the voice of a speaker) will divert your attention from your own thoughts and help your conscious brain switch off.

In Japan they build nap rooms into some office buildings. How cool is that? If you work for a company outside Japan, though, and you don't think asking your boss to build a nap room for you would go down too well, try to find a place where you can sit during your break (please don't tell me you don't take breaks!) with your eyes closed for 20 minutes, put your phone on silent and listen to some music.

The more you rest, the better the quality of everything you touch will be. It is as simple as that.

GIVE

I find that the more I give the more I receive. I have no idea how it works, but what I do know is that it does work! Some stuff you don't need to figure out. I used to try to understand everything; I spent hours contemplating all the 'whys'. I used to wonder how come ungrateful people are ungrateful, for example. Now I know: because they're ungrateful. What else would you expect them to be?

Giving is great and as for the receiving part, it comes from all directions, not necessarily from the person we gave something to. You will notice it if you pay attention.

It doesn't have to be about money or things. It can be a smile to a stranger or asking a friend, 'How are you?' and actually mean it. Offer your time to someone, give a gift of active listening (that's the one when you don't check your phone throughout the conversation). Pay attention to how you feel when you give. Studies have shown that both giver and receiver benefit emotionally from the act of giving, and so does an observer. Isn't that fascinating?

Try and give something today without expecting any recognition.

STOP CRITICISING YOURSELF

Most often we are our own biggest critics; nobody is as harsh on us as we are on ourselves. Why is that? Why would we discourage the one person we should keep encouraging the most?

Also, when we do it in front of other people, we automatically give them the idea that's it's ok to criticise us. It's not. We teach people how to treat us by example; we need to pay close attention to what we teach them.

Be kind to yourself.

DO WHAT YOU WANT TO DO

Why? Because it's your life. It's not your parents' life or your partner's life, it's yours. Deep inside, you often know what you want, but because there are so many other voices around you it's sometimes really hard to hear the most important voice coming from within.

People who have gained significant things in life are not the types who wait for somebody's approval before doing something. They just went for it, and if it didn't go as planned, they just dealt with the consequences.

It takes courage, of course. It takes balls. But you can either find them (the balls) and live your life on your terms, leading it the way you want, or follow someone else's idea for your life – the choice is yours.

I quit school when I was 17 and, let me tell you, quitting school in Poland where I come from is not the same as quitting school in the UK or the States. Nobody quits school in Poland, definitely not someone who, after being exceptionally good in primary school, got to one of the best high schools in one of the biggest cities and was on track to get a place in just about any university. That country is all about education and even people with several degrees struggle to get a decent job. So it certainly wasn't easy for me, moneywise, until I came to London, to what I think is the best city in the world, aged 22.

My parents almost had heart attacks when they found out. It took them over 10 years to accept that their son wouldn't have a degree simply because he didn't care about having one.

Looking back, although very unpopular, it was one of the best decisions I've ever made. I've never regretted it, not even for a split second. The only thing I regret is that I didn't do it when I was 16. I just didn't have the balls to face my parents then.

Since the day I left school, I haven't stopped learning. Academic education didn't do it for me; self-education certainly did. Learning what I wanted, how I wanted and when I wanted.

What is it that you want? And if you aren't yet acting on it, why not? What, or who, is holding you back?

We only get one shot in life, don't we? One shot only.

BE AN APPRECIATOR

One of my favourite personal development exercises is something called a gratitude list. You list all the things (minimum of 20 items) you're grateful for at the end of each day. What a fantastic alternative it is to going through all the things that went wrong that day, don't you think? Oprah Winfrey gave a massive credit to this exercise for helping her go from poverty to wealth. Or you could try the method Tim Ferriss uses. Every morning he listens to a song of his choice and as he exhales he thinks about one thing in his life he's grateful for. That's something you could easily do in your car (possibly with your eyes open) or in the train on your way to work. The 'how' is secondary, just find a way that works best for you.

If you can't appreciate what you have already you might struggle to get more out of life, but more than that, if you can't appreciate what you have you will never be fully happy, and what's more important than being happy?

I've noticed that I'm much more likely to give something (a compliment, a favour, a little gift) again to someone who expressed a genuine appreciation when I gave him or her something for the first time. It's so much easier to give to appreciators, isn't it? Learn to be an appreciator to get the most out of people and life in general.

GO DATING

A big part of my coaching has always been in the area of relationships, not because I chose it that way, but because it's such an important area of our lives.

My single clients are rarely happy to be single, and the ones who are not single are rarely not facing some relationship challenges they would like to discuss with me.

If you're single and that's not because you want it that way right now, just go and date. If nothing else, you will make new friends! The world belongs to people who are proactive.

BE PERSISTENT, DON'T GIVE UP

One of the three fundamentals of success (the other two are right belief and taking action) is persistence. No skill worth having has been acquired by practising something once or twice. It's been said that it takes about 10,000 hours to master a high level craft. We don't all necessarily want to be masters in something, but it's important to realise that achieving anything does take time and require lots of persistence.

We can look at a fantastic pianist on the stage or an Olympic athlete and think they're just talented. They are talented, but they've also spent thousands of hours practising their craft, possibly even more than their colleagues, which is why they are the ones we are watching.

Don't give up because you tried once and it didn't work out as well as you imagined it would, or because one random person told you shouldn't be doing it. Keep going, keep on pushing.

The bamboo tree takes five years of watering before it shows anything above the ground at all. Five years! But when it starts to grow, it grows up 20 metres in one year. Many things in life are just like this tree.

Occasionally, there is a time to give up and move on; this is a personal story to illustrate it. I call it the 'Trumpet Story'.

I've always loved music. I remember listening to Beethoven on cassettes (do you remember cassettes?) when I was a kid. My dad took me for private classical guitar lessons when I was aged seven. I was going to see the teacher once a week for six months, but it didn't go down very well. It might have something to do with the fact the guitar I was playing on was bigger than me.

When I was 16 I took the very same guitar from under the bed and taught myself how to play it. After practising basic chords relentlessly in my room, within a few months I was singing and playing in front of my high school class and then the whole school. I was good.

Then one day I went to a concert of the best Polish jazz guitar player. It hit me, and it hit me hard. I left having fallen totally in love with jazz. I forgot about playing rock/pop songs on the guitar and became obsessed: Miles Davis, John Coltrane, Chick Corea, Keith Jarrett were the sound of my teenage years. I decided to play the trumpet myself, but not just that; I decided to become the best trumpet player on the planet.

There was no jazz school in my city so I had to go to the evening classical music school. My plan was to learn how to use the instrument there and work on jazz harmonies myself. What a love affair that was, the trumpet and me. I would spend every spare minute practising. Within a few months I was improvising with a bunch of friends playing different instruments in our music school's basement rooms – some of the best moments of my life.

Everything went well for several months until I started to prepare for our first year final exam. I had serious difficulties hitting some high-pitched notes in the piece I was playing. The trumpet is an extremely physical instrument: you play eight different notes using your lips and the muscles around your lips only, and generate all the rest with the three valves on the top.

I spent countless hours preparing, but I knew very well that something wasn't right. I started to play in front of the examiners and, when that highest note came, I totally blew it. Finishing the piece after that was mental torture. 'Can you leave us for a minute, please,' one of them said.

When I entered the room, all three of them had their heads down and looked as if someone had just died. You could cut the tension with a knife. Nobody wanted to say anything, then my trumpet teacher told me that this was my first and last year in the school.

For a second the world stopped. Tears came to my eyes, but I managed to hold them back until I left the room.

The one thing I wanted to do with my life had just been taken away from me.

Then, while I was in the toilet crying, an idea came to my head. Miles Davis had died in 1991 so I couldn't go and see him. It was 2000 and the best jazz trumpet player alive was the Polish jazz star, Tomasz Stanko. I would go and see him; if he could tell me there was something I could do I would do it, if not, I would never play the trumpet again.

Somehow I got his address and phone number, but I couldn't get him on the phone. I decided to travel to his house in Warsaw with a friend.

After eight hours in the train, we arrived at Warsaw's central station on a hot summer's day. After trying various ways, Stanko eventually agreed to see me.

'Play the sound,' he said as I entered the spacious living room. I opened the suitcase, took out my trumpet and played a long sound. 'Forget about it,' he said. 'Your lips and the muscles around them are not made for playing the trumpet.'

Some things are just not meant to be. Move on. There might be something even greater waiting for you around the corner. In my case, that 'greater' thing was what I'm doing right now.

ANTICIPATE GREAT THINGS WILL HAPPEN

You know the morning when you wake up, something goes wrong – you start the day with cornflakes and you realise there is no more milk, for example – and you think to yourself, 'Shit, it's only going to get worse from here.' What kind of day do you usually get after that: not too good, right? If you anticipate having a bad day, that's exactly what you're likely to get.

On the other hand, if you wake up thinking it's going to be a great day, you will be rarely disappointed.

I have conditioned myself to break the spell every time something like the 'cornflakes' situation takes place. Instead of going for a 'what's next, will the trains be cancelled as well?' mindset, as I would have done in the past, I now think to myself, 'ok, it's just the milk, only the milk, no big deal'. Treating each incident as a one-off prevents a snowball effect of negative expectation developing. Try it, it works like magic. Don't let your attitude control you; learn to control your attitude.

For years I've been anticipating great things will happen to me and, guess what? They do, all the time.

DREAM BIG

We achieve many of our dreams. The problem is we usually don't dream big enough, so once we achieve them they don't really excite us. As Michelangelo put it, 'The greater danger for most of us is not that our aim is too high and we miss it, but that is too low and we hit it.'

Dream big, my friends, get excited by your vision. The more your vision turns you on, the easier and more enjoyable the journey towards getting what you want will be.

Don't limit your life from being what it can be.

CHART YOUR PROGRESS

To achieve your dreams, all you need is measurable progress in reasonable time.

It's essential that we measure our progress so we know that we are getting somewhere. If you are working on your fitness goals, for instance, you should weigh and measure yourself once a week.

If we chart our progress towards all our goals, we can see relatively quickly when one approach isn't working as well as it could be; that it might be time to go about things in a different way. On the other hand, if things are working and we can clearly see that, it empowers us to keep going.

BREAKFAST LIKE A KING, DINE LIKE A BEGGAR

One of the biggest mistakes I see many people making in their eating habits is skipping breakfast.

Breakfast should be the biggest (calorie-wise) meal of the day for three important reasons:

1. It kick starts our metabolism – crucial if you're trying to lose weight

2. It gives your muscles protein after eight hours of starvation – crucial if you're trying to put on or even maintain your muscle tissue

3. It gives your brain the energy to function at its best – crucial if you want to be really productive at work

A bowl of muesli won't cut it; high protein eggs, salmon, spinach and avocado combined will.

'But I'm not hungry in the morning,' I hear you saying. Of course you're not if you eat a lot before going to bed. Which leads me to the next point: don't eat anything at least two hours, and up to four hours before going to sleep, particularly any carbohydrates (pasta, rice, bread, sweets etc). Carbohydrates equal energy and energy equals trouble falling asleep and as you won't have the opportunity to burn them during the night, your body will store them as fat.

Most of people make the mistake of eating very little in the morning and a lot in the evening. It should be the other way around. If you're one of them, turn it around and see the difference in how you feel in no time!

LEARN TO TAKE CRITICISM

There is nothing better than constructive criticism. I know that now; I didn't understand that until I was in my early twenties. We can learn so much from it.

I wish more people had the courage to constructively criticise me without me actually having to ask for it. I can't really blame my friends for the fact that they don't want to hurt my feelings; what they don't know is that they wouldn't because I see it as something positive, something serving my growth. Let's embrace everything that helps us to become the best we can possibly be, even if it may slightly hurt our egos sometimes.

Criticism (the not so constructive kind), on the other hand, is something we will never avoid and the more successful we become in anything, the more of it we're going to experience. You know you're doing well when people start to criticise you. I am currently being criticised a few times a month. I am trying to get this increased to a few times a week and then maybe even a few times a day. You think I'm kidding? I'm actually not. It's better to be criticised than to be ignored.

We need to grow a thick skin and a positive response to receiving criticism because the only alternatives are to keep getting offended and not knowing how we can up our game. I don't know about you, but that doesn't sound too exciting to me.

FIND YOUR PASSION

Occasionally your passion will find you, but if you're waiting for it to arrive, you might as well try to find it yourself.

My biggest passion by far is, and has been for many years, personal development. I'm fascinated by the whole idea of bettering ourselves. I spent a few years working on all aspects of my life with tremendous results. Then, an amazing thing happened. One beautiful morning, I was in my bed watching a YouTube video of Tony Robbins, one of the big boys in my industry, and it hit me: the idea of turning my passion into a career.

It hit me so hard I could barely sleep for the next three days.

It was like love at first sight.

Within minutes, I knew beyond any doubt that I was going to spend the rest of my life helping people to become the best versions of themselves, just like I had helped myself already. Since then, that thought has never left me.

I know I'm extremely fortunate. I'm grateful for it every day. It felt as though my passion had found me – but if I had not been working on what interested me, the passion that is now my career would not have occurred to me.

Instead of waiting for your passion to find you, ask yourself these questions:

- If I could do one thing for the rest of my life, what would it be?
- What do I love to do?
- What would I do, even if I didn't get paid to do it?

Go deep within, think about what you love to do with your spare time.

If you struggle to find anything straight away, go and try some new interests or activities. Talk to people who are involved with what you find interesting. Expose yourself to opportunities. Explore!

Find your passion and you will never have to 'work' for one more day in your life. I haven't for years. It's like winning the lottery.

DON'T BE AFRAID
TO MAKE MISTAKES

That would mean a lifetime of being afraid because, no matter how smart and experienced we become, we will always keep making mistakes. As long as we don't make the same mistakes over and over again, we're good. Making mistakes equals being human, so go easy on yourself next time it happens.

The list of mistakes I have made in my life is as long as my arm. Two arms actually. And one or two legs. Some of them were colossal. They made me who I am today and if I had to make them all to be who I am today, it was worth it. Don't forget, we learn nowhere near as much from our successes as we do from our mistakes.

Successful people make as many mistakes as everybody else; they just deal with them very differently by not making a big deal of them, and putting the learning to good use. The only proven method to avoid mistakes is to do nothing. But then, doing nothing is the biggest mistake of all, as far as I'm concerned, so there is no escape from it.

Be bold, go for what you believe in and welcome the mistakes you will make on your way as a part of your learning curve. Don't dread them, embrace them.

REVIEW YOUR LIFE

Every now and then you need to review your life to see where you are and where would you like to be. With the latter, no matter how sure you might be about your goals today, they may be different the day after tomorrow based on what happens or doesn't happen tomorrow.

The best time for reviews is when we are on holiday. It is so much easier to look at our life and get a clearer perspective when we are outside it. I personally like to review my life at the end of each year, look back, compare it to the year before and think about how to make the following year even better.

DON'T TRY TO BE PERFECT

Why? Because that will lead to a life full of disappointment. There is no such thing as being perfect in anything or for anybody. You can spend years trying to fully please your boss or partner and the chances are you will never do it.

What's the alternative, then? Try to be as good as you can be and if you're the best you can be and someone is not happy with it, well, let them not be happy with it. I find that one of the many common characteristics of really happy people is that they don't try to be perfect.

I like what Voltaire said: 'Don't let the perfect be the enemy of the good.' Most often, good or especially very good, is really good enough.

IMAGE DOES COUNT

Ok, so people shouldn't judge us based on our appearance, but guess what? They do. Constantly. Maybe unconsciously, but still.

Would I say it's the most important thing out there? No, because if you don't know what you're talking about a tailored suit isn't going to help you, but out of all the things that can sell us short, image is the easiest one to fix.

One big thing is grooming: looking neat and tidy every time we go beyond our local store. One of my ex-girlfriends would say that she wouldn't even take the rubbish out without makeup on. Having said that, I don't remember her taking rubbish out... ever. And I certainly didn't need makeup to do so.

Another thing is the clothes we wear: their quality, how they fit and whether or not their colour matches our complexion. As for the latter, I've only recently learnt about that from my lovely stylist friend. In the past I just thought that if I didn't feel good wearing certain colours it was because I just didn't like those particular colours. Little did I know, different colours or, to be more precise, different shades of colours, match different combinations of our skin, hair and eye colour.

For a long time my friend tried to convince me that there were better colours for me than the black and white I always wore (there was really no difference whether you took a colour or a black-and-white picture of me; as they looked exactly the same). After something called colour analysis, where she put various samples of shades of colours next to my face, I went absolutely crazy and expanded my palette to grey and navy. She tried very hard and, to be honest, I could see that certain shades of pink, for example, are good for my complexion; I'm just not ready for it yet. Maybe one day. Right, who am I kidding?

95% of the first impression we make on others is supposedly with the clothes we wear. Why? Because clothes cover 95% of our body.

STOP BEING JEALOUS

I'm not talking about a little jealousy in a relationship here. That's inevitable if you really love someone, for most of us, myself included, anyway. I'm talking about feeling or showing envy of someone or their achievements. It's not constructive and it takes our focus away from what's most important – our own progress.

I personally love to see other people doing well, if they do ten times better than me, fine! First of all, it's good to see them happy; second of all, other people's success motivates me to do better myself.

I sometimes hear my clients saying that they envy other people and don't like this trait in themselves. Self-awareness is the first step towards eliminating this unproductive feeling; making a firm decision to stop it is the second, and often final, one.

LEARN TO PLAN

Do you know the saying, 'Failing to plan is planning to fail'? We should have as many plans as possible: a plan for a day, for a week, month, year; a fitness plan if we work on our fitness; a financial plan if we run a business.

I make lots of my clients write a plan for the next day before they leave their office. The more senior they are, the more important it becomes as forgetting things costs more with greater responsibility. Then weekly plans on Sunday (they don't like me very much for this idea, I have to say, and no wonder I don't get Christmas cards from their partners). Daily planning takes 5-10 minutes; weekly plans take up to an hour. The thing is, the benefits well surpass the time committed to it.

The number one reason why lots of people quit gyms around February, after signing up for it in

January as part of their New Year's resolutions, is because they don't have a plan. It's really hard to stick to something if you don't know what you're doing or where you're heading. You get discouraged and quit.

And remember, a decent plan that you follow is way better than a fantastic one you don't.

STOP WORRYING

There are only two kinds of things we can worry about: things we can't control and things we can control. If we can't control something, why should we worry about it? And if we can control it, why would we worry if we can still change it?

Ok, I won't even try to pretend I don't worry about anything anymore, but I feel like I have it well under control. What I mean by that is worry doesn't stop me from taking action towards what I want, it's just there in the background sometimes.

If you worry a lot it may be because when you were young people around you were worrying so you worried a little too. Then you may have progressed to worrying a little bit more, then a little bit more and before you knew it, you became a habitual worrier and now it is just a part of who you are.

What's the way out of it, then? Start by committing to going through one day without worrying – every time you are about to do it, change your focus, think of something else and just don't do it. Easier said than done, I know. There is no other way though. We change the habit of doing something by... not doing it. And then this not doing it becomes a new habit, something natural.

SET REMINDERS

My memory is very good, but my memory supported by reminders is excellent. We live in a world full of amazing technology and I don't know about you, but I like to take full advantage of it.

I set reminders on the phone app and now, even better, Siri (iPhone's personal assistant) is setting them for me. I love Siri, but when I asked her whether she loves me too, she left me hanging with a 'Let me get back to you on that'. I'm still waiting, by the way.

NON-VERBAL COMMUNICATION IS KEY

Only 7% of our communication is verbal yet we give so much importance to the words. I say, let's continue giving importance to them but pay much more attention to our voice tonality (38%) and particularly our body language (the remaining 55% of communication).

If a mother says, 'Come here, I love you' to a child, in a serious voice while standing stiffly with her arms crossed and a stern expression on her face, which message do you think will be stronger to the child?

Another thing very high status people (country leaders, top CEOs) have in common is their great control over voice tonality and body language. They usually achieve this with the help of coaches.

There are two elements of voice tonality: pace and pitch.

Notice that all high status people speak at a slow pace. Why? They know they are high status and if you are high status you don't need to rush with anything, people will wait for you to finish your sentence or speech, no matter how boring you are.

We don't need to become U.S. presidents to speak as slowly as they do and therefore make more impact in our interactions with those around us. So take your time when you speak, pause a lot.

As for the pitch, try to sound as low as you can for maximum effect.

Body language starts with posture. Whether you walk, stand or sit, keep your head up, your shoulders straight and chest up.

When you shake someone's hand, don't just touch it – shake it. A weak handshake won't impress anybody. Use it as your advantage, you can make yourself look more confident than you actually are by going for a strong handshake (in a job interview scenario, for instance), especially if you combine it with a strong, but friendly, eye contact. I don't know about you, but I personally have a problem in trusting people who don't look me in the eye when we talk (I forgive them when we talk on the phone, most of the time anyway).

Eye contact is more important in building rapport than anything you can ever say.

Last but not least, use your hands when you speak; gesture, but don't touch your face unless there is a genuine reason for it; don't make any unnecessary body movements, period. They're all signs of nervousness.

Be aware of the concept of open body language and closed body language. The latter is when we cross our legs and particularly our arms. It makes us appear cold and unfriendly.

An experiment where 50% of participants were asked to listen to a lecture with closed body language and 50% with open body language. The latter group ended up remembering 38% more from the lecture. Fascinating!

GET INSPIRED

I always have surrounded myself with people who inspire me, 'real' people as well as teachers and mentors I've never met (and never will as many of them are dead). I have to say that I fall asleep with men more often than I do with women. I'm talking about personal growth speakers I listen to at bedtime. I let them go on for hours after I fall asleep. I know that even though the conscious part of my brain is asleep, my subconscious keeps receiving what they say.

Revisit the movies that inspired you. If they had the power to do it once, they have the potential to do it again and again and again. There are certain films I've watched many times over the years. Why? Because they really inspire me. *Forrest Gump, Dead Poets Society, Jerry McGuire, Good Will Hunting* and *Rain Man* to name a few. What movies do it for you?

Don't forget the books, quotes and places. Create a database and keep revisiting them as you look around for new sources of inspiration.

FORGIVE

I love what Gandhi said: 'The weak can never forgive. Forgiveness is the attribute of the strong.'

I remember thinking when I was younger, 'I'm a man, of course I can't forgive'. Now I think, 'I'm a man, of course I forgive'. I remember, but I forgive. I might cut someone from my life if I have to, but in peace and without any feeling of resentment. People let me down all the time (most often on a microscale only) and I'm sure that, despite all the effort (and I'm also sure there could be more effort sometime), I let them down too sometimes. I choose to see the best in people and guess what I end up seeing. Plenty of good and little of 'not so good'.

Think about it, if you hate somebody, that person usually doesn't care. Most of the time they won't even know you hate them. Who are you hurting? Yourself, and yourself only. What's the point of carrying anger about anything or anyone? Where does it lead?

If someone cheated on you, for example, whether or not you forgive them you have been cheated on and that's not going to change, so why not forgive and save yourself from carrying resentment for months, if not years, or a lifetime, to come.

And there is self-forgiveness. Start with this one if you can. I have made mistakes in my life so ridiculous you wouldn't believe them. If I can forgive myself for those poor choices and misjudgements, you can forgive yourself for yours, whatever they are, too. If I can have a resentment-free life, so can you.

Make the decision to forgive yourself and others today.

LOVE YOURSELF

One of the many things I love about living in London is the variety of different nationalities here. Meeting so many people from so many parts of the world has made me realise how incredibly similar we are at the core.

The relationship you have with yourself is the only relationship you're ever going to be able to be 100% certain of. You are the only person who can't possibly break up with you, cheat on you, move away from you; the only person you can't even have a short break from. If that's the case, why would you consider, even for a split second, not making the quality of this relationship your top priority.

If we don't love ourselves we can't truly love anybody else. How can we give something we don't have? Start with yourself and see how much easier it will be to extend love to others. People will be drawn to you because you won't be seeking their validation. Why? Because you will have plenty of it already. You will stop going around asking for acceptance; you will be happy to give acceptance wherever you go.

I find that the least happy people are those who most lack self-love. Not money, not relationships – self-love. Change your own negative thought patterns, your concept of yourself, and spend more time with people who make you feel good about yourself as opposed to those who don't. Do more things you're good at and invest your time and energy in self-growth – the best investment you will ever make.

Start the love affair with yourself today.

BE YOURSELF

There are three very powerful questions you can ask yourself in order to become clearer about your own identity. They are also some of the most difficult questions you can ever ask yourself, so if you're reading this standing on a crowded bus, for example, you might want to wait until you're back home with a cup of tea or a glass of wine, and attempt to answer them then.

The first one is 'Who am I?'

We need to know who we are to be ourselves.

The second is 'What do I want?'

And the third is 'Where am I going?'

A big part in the process of being yourself is to stop caring about how other people perceive you and consequently stop taking things personally. There is an art to it. Most of us want other people to like us, accept us and appreciate us, but if we change ourselves to please others or to avoid possible criticism, we stop being true to who we are.

I used to wonder why not everybody liked me, how come not everybody gets me. I would try to round some edges to get more approval from more people. I don't do it anymore. My attitude now is that if you like me and get me that's great, but if you don't, that's ok, too. I've learnt that no matter who we are, what we do and how we do it, some people will just not like us and, if that's the case, we might as well be true to who we are at all times.

I like to think that if two of the most loving, caring and empathetic men this world has ever seen – Jesus and Gandhi – had so many critics, what chance do I have of not having any.

We should be independent from the good opinions of other people, cultivate positive beliefs about ourselves, stop comparing ourselves to others, follow our own style, whatever it is, and fully express our individuality.

'Be yourself; everyone else is already taken,' as Oscar Wilde put it.

HAVE ROLE MODELS IN LIFE

I find having role models incredibly useful. If we're lucky, we can model ourselves on our parents; if we're not so lucky, we can use them as reverse role models – as the kind of people we don't want to end up being.

I was very fortunate in being able to learn very different things from my parents. How to love, give and be empathetic from my mum, and how not to take shit from anybody from my dad. Then when I was 13, my ju-jitsu instructor became my role model for the three years I was trained by him. The guy was the ultimate man for me: not only was he intelligent, fun and strong, I also liked his girlfriend a lot. 'I wanna be like him when I grow up,' I remember thinking.

Who were your first role models?

Whatever you want to do in life, whatever industry you're in, modelling yourself on the top people in that field will help you succeed faster. Someone has been there, done that; you can follow their steps and avoid mistakes they've made.

A practical tip is that even while you have one eye on the top person in your industry, keep the other eye on the person just above you. If they are doing what you would like to be doing in a year or two's time, they will be easier to access and therefore to model.

FOLLOW YOUR HEART

Whether you call it heart, intuition or gut feeling, I believe that voice has the answers to most of our questions. The problem is, our mind and other people's minds produce so much 'noise' it's sometimes hard to hear it.

Notice that every time you try to make a decision you will receive multiple opinions and much advice. We all get to choose which one to follow; occasionally they're in sync –no dilemma in that case. If they are not in sync, I like to go with my gut feeling. That way I'm convinced that I'm accessing something bigger than myself. Over the years, I've learnt to trust my intuition more than anything or anybody else.

DON'T SETTLE FOR LESS THAN YOU CAN GET

Let's use an example of something that is easy to count – money. If you're on £20,000 a year and your capacity is to be on £20,000 a year, there's no problem. There is no shame in it. You go to work, work hard (or not so hard) and get your pay cheque at the end of the month covering, hopefully, your basic needs. If your capacity is to earn £100,000 a year, though, that's an entirely different story as you are just not achieving your full potential (financial and perhaps other potential).

I met this amazing young guy who had a full-time job paying the minimum wage. He got so used to it (we can get used to just about anything, can't we?), he didn't see anything unusual or inappropriate about it. I told him I thought he was wasting his considerable potential and made him look for a better job.

It's painful for me to see great people settling for less than they can get. They will often have a good story to explain why, but I refuse to buy it.

Are you maximising your potential? Are you earning as much as you could have right now? If you're in a relationship, are you being the best partner you can be? On the other side of the coin, is your partner as good as you want them to be or have you just settled for less thinking it's the best you'll ever get?

If the answers to these, or similar questions, are negative ones, don't think too much about it; thinking doesn't change much, as we know. Act on it, do something about it. What are you waiting for?

One of the biggest problems we face is something called the upper limit problem. We think there is a limit to what we can get. Using the first example - money, there will be a limit in some cases, some exceptions. Let's say someone has two brain cells, no people skills and refuses to play the lottery. The chances of that person ever becoming a millionaire are rather slim.

I was fortunate enough not to have the upper limit in this department, when it came to my love life though, it was an entirely different story.

For years I believed I could only date a certain type of woman thinking that I'm not good enough to date the ones that I really liked. Through personal development I realised that it wasn't the reality (as I thought previously), it was only my perception of reality created by my limiting mind at the time.

Gaining this level of awareness was the first step towards crashing that old belief and replacing it with the conviction that not only can I have passion for what I do, the best friends one could ask for, all the money I ever want, but also, I can date just about whoever I want.

I've learnt that I don't ever need to settle for less than I think I can get in anything. I became a no-limit person. And because I became a no-limit person myself (remembering where I came from), I find it very easy to convince others about their potential that they don't take full advantage of.

STOP WATCHING THE NEWS

Why? Because it's depressing.

Unless your work requires you to know what's going on locally or around the world I'm asking you, why are you doing it to yourself? Pay attention and notice how even five minutes' exposure to news will affect your mental state, notice how incredibly difficult it will be to feel happy after five minutes of murders, rapes and other drama.

I believe there are a million acts of kindness for every act of hatred in the world. I see people being kind to other people every single day. Watching the news is like watching the events from some other planet for me. It provides us with such a distorted vision of the world, one could think (one who never leaves the house or stops watching news) that it's all bad out there, whereas 'bad' is just a fraction of everything else.

SMILE

Smiling is the best ice-breaker, rapport-builder and communication tool known to humanity. We can say more with one genuine smile which reaches up to our eyes than many words. Plus, it doesn't cost us anything!

Start smiling more and see how dramatically your interactions with people change.

DO WHAT YOU LOVE

If you could wake up tomorrow and do anything, what would it be? Don't worry how much it pays or what your friends or relatives would think about it. What would it be?

Once you answer that, do everything, but I mean, everything, to make that thing your career. Sell the house, change all your friends, learn another language and go to another country, move mountains if you have to. Trust me, lying on your deathbed you won't be thankful for having played it safe, having stuck to the job you disliked for 30 years. You will feel a massive regret for not having done what you really wanted to.

I was working in fashion retail, leading teams of up to 50 people, when I discovered coaching (or when coaching discovered me, as it felt).

I was quite good at it, but I certainly didn't love it. Do you think the career transition was easy for me? Do you think everything went smoothly and I didn't get stressed out? Nope, unfortunately not. Despite the fact I knew I wanted to coach, I couldn't just quit my retail job.

I started to coach part-time and I'd been doing it for a year, trying to save up some money to make the transition feasible, when I was made redundant.

I started looking for another job to pay the rent, but strangely enough I couldn't find one. I say 'strangely' because I had never had this problem before. After two months I got really close to a job with Prada. I told myself that if I didn't get it I would quit looking and push my coaching business full-time. I didn't get it, fortunately, and within four months I went from having one client to having 20 clients, running five talks per week and generating 150% of my retail income.

How did it happen?

It wasn't luck, or the fact that someone gave me something to make it easy for me. I've worked my ass off, that's what happened. Dedication, commitment, hours spent on learning (marketing, sales, advertising, public speaking, you name it), pushing, pushing, pushing. Creating something with no financial backing, driving it with passion and the vision of the future I wanted, with the support of my friends and family.

Looking back, I know I've achieved something remarkable, and it's only got better. But what I also know is that if I could do it, so can you. I'm not special, I just love what I do and that love made the seemingly impossible (or highly unlikely) possible. I had the motivation to find solutions to all the challenges I encountered, answers to all the questions I had. I couldn't afford any mentors or coaches back then.

If you're passionate about something, you will find a way to get where you need to get to.

One more thing, as love is what drives your business forward, don't even think about working for yourself unless you truly love what you want to do. Why? Because there will be times it's going to be really tough, the phone won't ring, clients will quit on you, you will feel low, and the only thing that will keep you going will be that love.

Howard Thurman said: 'Ask not what the world needs. Instead, ask what makes you come alive and go do that, as what world needs are people who come alive.'

BUILD ON SMALL SUCCESSES

Whatever you do, have the big picture in mind at all times: the vision, the end goal. But what you must focus on is the next step in front of you that will lead to one small success, and then the next step and success and then the next.

Collect all the little wins, as they are what big success is built on; the hundreds or thousands of things you do every day, decisions you make, people you talk to. Don't try to run before you can walk, be patient with yourself.

CHALLENGE YOUR FEARS

The biggest fear out there is that of public speaking. 52% of the population has it, that's more than fear of heights and flying.

I remember well my very first public speaking event, I was nervous as hell. The fear disappeared as I ran more and more of them and now, over 200 events later, it's as easy as talking to a friend. Having said that, when I got invited to speak to an audience of over 100 people for the first time, I felt fearful again. Most events I had run up to that point were for groups of up to 20 people and, because part of me was afraid of it, I knew I had to do it. I did have a shaky start but, you know what, next time I spoke to a large group I was a little less nervous, then after another few times it was like talking to a friend again. When I'm invited to speak to 500 people the cycle will start all over again because that's just the way it is.

To continue with the example of public speaking, you can't get rid of the fear by reading a book on public speaking. The only way to get rid of the fear of public speaking is to speak publicly. There is no shortcut. If you're afraid of something you have to confront it to stop being afraid. And the more often you confront it, the more comfortable you will become doing it.

Identify your fears, and then face them one by one. Live a fear-free life. I can't wait for that invite to speak to a massive audience; I can't wait to face the very few of my remaining fears.

USE YOUR IMAGINATION

Einstein said that 'imagination is more important than knowledge'. I don't know about you, but if one of the greatest scientists who's ever lived says something, I will at least seriously consider it may be true.

Visualisation is one of the most powerful personal development exercises. It is used to imagine all the things that you want in your life. An interesting fact is that our subconscious brain cannot differentiate between the actual events and the events we have only imagined.

We can use our imagination to take us a step closer to our goals. It's very simple: it has to start with the vision, and the stronger the vision (the more real it appears in our head), the better. If you think about a house with a big garden in the South of France, feel the warmth of the sun and smell the flowers you will have in this garden.

If you think about an Italian supercar, hear the roar of its engine, feel what it's like to sit in the driver's seat and hold the steering wheel.

Think about the things you desire in the last five minutes before you fall asleep – the most important five minutes of your day. Your subconscious will marinate for the next eight hours whatever you were thinking about then. We often spend this time going through all the things that could have gone better during the day; how much better to spend the last five minutes of the day visualising the future you want. Try it for a week, starting today. The power of imagination is huge.

IT'S ALL ABOUT RESULTS

I don't respect hard working people only because they work hard. Not unless they produce results. What's better, working hard and having nothing, or not working at all and having nothing? At least with the latter you're not tired at the end of the day.

A few questions to ask yourself:

- Is there a bigger plan behind the hours I put into doing something?
- Is there an easier, faster, more enjoyable or more productive way of achieving the same thing?
- Can I outsource some of my work?

We want to use our brain here to get as much done to the highest possible standard with the smallest effort so we can use the remaining energy to do other stuff. We want to work hard at working smart.

Results is the name of the game, so no matter what you do or how you do it, make sure you produce results (even if they're tiny to begin with) otherwise you're just wasting your time and energy.

THINK SOLUTIONS

There is a solution to almost any problem. Whether we see it or not, it's there. I like dealing with problems because I take joy in the process of coming up with the solutions. As I come up with them for a living, over the years I've conditioned my mind to produce them fast.

I meet a prospective client for the first time and as they are talking about the challenges they face my brain is inevitably entering the solution-finding mode. By the time they ask me, 'Do you think you can help?' I can usually say with a smile. 'I don't think I can, I know I can.'

My clients (and people in general) often think their problems are unique. They're not; they are unique as individuals but their problems – or, as I prefer to call them, opportunities – are universal.

When it comes to solutions, it doesn't matter how we find them, whether we find them ourselves, ask a friend, ask a friend to ask his friends, hire a professional, google or youtube the answer (we live in wonderful times when what we need is often only a click away, don't we?).

UNDERSTAND YOUR MIND

Our mind isn't always our best friend. It can be our worst enemy until we learn how to manage it. Note that our brain's main job is to avoid trouble and risk; to protect us so we can produce as many offspring as possible. Survival and pursuing great things in life don't always go hand in hand.

Every time we try to do something that puts us at any risk whatsoever (which is every time we go outside our comfort zone), our mind will give us all the possible reasons why we shouldn't be doing it. Things like: 'Who do you think you are?', 'What makes you think you can do it?', 'Be careful, you're going to hurt yourself!' and all that crap. It's crap because it's not true. So many people never leave their comfort zone because of this inner voice. It's like this constant civil war between you (your unlimited potential, what you really want) and your mind.

One of the biggest differences between successful and unsuccessful people is not big potential v small potential, it's that the former learnt how to keep pushing forward despite the limiting voice coming from the inside.

You can never make the voice go away – and there are times when it really is necessary to your survival. You just need to learn when you should override its negative messages in order to achieve your goals.

So next time you hear that little voice, just tell it to shut up.

STOP MAKING EXCUSES

I love saying, 'If you really want to do something, you will find a way. If you don't, you will find an excuse'.

'I'm too short', 'I'm too old', 'I'm not smart enough', 'I don't have enough money', 'I don't have enough time'… the list goes on. If we look for an excuse we will always, always find one.

The truth is that these days we can't blame either our DNA or our brains as two new branches of science, epigenetics and neuroplasticity, tell us we can alter the structure of both.

For every excuse you can think of, I have a story of a client who was in the same or worse situation than you and achieved the thing you want to achieve.

Recognise that excuses are just that – excuses. They are only valid reasons to stop us from growing if we think they are, or if we let them be.

TRY NEW THINGS

As I'm writing this, I'm reminding myself about the importance of trying new things instead of always going for the things we are familiar with. Some people have a natural desire to constantly experiment with new music, cuisines, travel destinations etc. I personally would listen to the same music, eat the same food and not travel at all if I hadn't committed to trying new things as often as possible.

It's about expanding our horizons, seeing what's out there and learning about ourselves in the process.

IMPOSSIBLE DOESN'T EXIST

I want to tell you a story.

I remember very well when my girlfriend at the time came to my work a few years ago in tears. Her dad, due to heart problems, was in a coma in Slovakia, where she's from. Her dad was also the closest person to her. She was devastated. Doctors were saying his chance of coming round was slim and by law, they could only keep him connected to the life support machines for a month, unless someone paid 450 euros a week to extend it.

We didn't have this kind of money, nor did anyone in her family. She talked to doctors and to the director of the hospital; so did her lawyer. The hospital didn't seem to care.

She didn't tell me she had written a letter to the President until his office called.

The President, bless him, took matters into his own hands. He told the hospital's director not to disconnect her dad's life support without his personal authorisation and the whole thing started a national discussion about the situation of people in a coma.

Her dad never woke up. After a year and further health complications she decided to turn off his life support. The fact that she knew she had done everything she possibly could have made her loss a tiny bit easier. I should probably add that she was only 21 when she fought for her beloved dad's life.

There is so much more we could do if we only thought we were capable of doing it. You have the power to move mountains. Use this power.

IT STARTS WITH THE RIGHT BELIEF

Tony Robbins talks about 80% of success being mindset and the remaining 20% mechanics. I like the analogy he uses to describe how we create our beliefs.

Long before something becomes a belief, it's just an idea. Let's say a 15-year old boy approaches a girl at school and she rejects him in front of other people, laughing at him after she does it. He might think, 'Ok, it's just a one-off situation, it isn't a reflection on me or women in general'. He might. But he might think, 'I suck', or 'Women don't like me', or 'Women cannot be trusted'.

Let's say he goes for the latter and now he has an idea that 'women cannot be trusted'. Imagine this idea is like a table top and the experience he had is a table leg. The next day he's watching a movie in which the hero is being dumped by his girlfriend. 'Women definitely cannot be trusted,' he thinks and the idea from yesterday becomes an assumption today. And the table has two legs (two reference points).

Every new, similar experience he has adds another leg to that table and within a couple of years the table becomes very solid and his assumption has become a belief. A strong belief might then become an unshakeable conviction that 'women cannot be trusted', which is obviously nonsense, but so is the belief that you can't succeed financially during a recession, yet many people hold it.

So four phases: from idea to assumption to belief to conviction. The later the phase, the harder it is to override it as our mind always looks for the evidence to support the beliefs we have.

The thing is, no matter what we do or how we do it, if the belief that we can actually achieve it is not there, we will struggle. Using the above example, the man with the ridiculous belief that women cannot be trusted will struggle in his relationships until he gives up this belief.

The way I help my clients to replace negative, disempowering beliefs with positive, empowering ones is by questioning the reference points supporting the former and at the same time looking for the reference points supporting the latter.

We can change our beliefs about anything, sometimes in an instant (usually while experiencing something significant); more often, though, it's a process. Remember that we don't get what we want in life, we get what we believe we can get and that's a huge difference.

The most important beliefs determining our lives are those about ourselves, our own potential, and about the world in general. Einstein said: 'The most important decision we make is whether we believe we live in a friendly or hostile universe.' Whatever your belief on this one, you will find plenty of evidence around to support it, so why not go for the friendly universe?

MANAGE YOUR EXPECTATIONS

As Shakespeare said, 'There is nothing either good or bad but thinking makes it so.' The situation itself is never a problem, it's what we think about it. And we often have a negative take on a situation because our expectation is too high. We can only feel disappointed if the reality doesn't match our expectations.

How about working on ourselves, giving our best, but accepting things as they come without feeling disappointed? I appreciate it's one of the hardest things we can learn, but it's got to be worth trying.

KNOW YOUR STRENGTHS
AND WEAKNESSES

Write a list of your strengths and another of your weaknesses. Do it now. It's very important to know them, especially when you're trying to decide what to do career wise. You want a job that involves as many of your strengths as possible and as few weaknesses as possible. My chosen profession is perfect for me in that I can utilise the things I'm good at, such as people skills, empathy and intuition, and doesn't require what I'm not so good at or I just dislike, such as technical stuff or physical tasks.

I would recommend you only spend your time and energy working on your weaknesses if absolutely necessary because you'll be much better off using your time and energy to enhance your strengths.

If you do a good job at this, you may be able to pay someone else to take care of all the things you're not too good at or you simply don't like doing. Which are usually the same.

TAKE RISKS

I take risks constantly. Usually they're micro risks, but still. I see the road to success of any kind being full of risks of all sizes. It's just the way it is. Especially if you're thinking about working for yourself, make sure that you're prepared to take lots of risks.

The obvious reason why people don't want to take risks is because they don't want to fail, but it's through failure not through success that we become stronger and shape our character, so whether we succeed or fail we gain something.

I don't know about you, but I would rather regret that I did something than that I didn't. I don't want to go through life playing it safe, taking a month to make the smallest decision, rarely leaving my comfort zone.

Don't take the risk of not taking risks and end up having a mediocre life as a result.

RECOGNISE YOU ALWAYS HAVE A CHOICE

Listen, we always have a choice. Sometimes we can't see it but the choice is always there. You hate your job? Change it. You don't like the size of your body? Change it. You feel unhappy in your relationship? Break up.

'Yes, but it's not as simple as that,' I hear you saying. It is to me, so what does it tell us? This simplicity/complexity issue is neither easy or difficult. It's subjective: it's difficult for you if you believe it is, and if that's your belief you're absolutely right; and it's easy for me because I believe this stuff is easy and I'm also right. Now, the thing is that I'm happy with my life. Are you?

People come to me for many reasons, but the bottom line is change. I hugely respect everybody who contacts me about coaching because I immediately know I'm dealing with someone with 'I can do' attitude. They might not know how to do something themselves, but if they didn't believe that change was possible they wouldn't have contacted me in the first place.

When I meet someone on a personal level and listen to them talking about a problem they face, my first question is, 'What are you doing about it'. If all they are interested in is the problem, with no intention of doing anything about it, I'm out. If, on the other hand, they're trying to do something about it, I'm all ears, thinking about possible ways of helping them.

People out there want to help you but you have to make the first step, to show some degree of readiness.

No matter how seemingly hopeless the situation is, remember you always have a choice to do something about it, either in changing the situation itself or at the very least, your attitude towards it.

BE POSITIVE

I am – and have always been – a glass half-full kind of person. And I only surround myself with people that think this way or those who are willing to learn to think this way.

There is no guarantee that thinking positively will lead to greater results, but I can promise you that it will take you further than thinking negatively. Plus, being negative is just not fun – not fun for you and certainly not fun for people around you.

If you look for faults in things and people you will always find them. Why not look for the good stuff and find that instead?

Make no mistake, a positive approach to life alone won't cut it. Sitting on the sofa repeating, 'I'm rich, I'm rich, I'm rich' will not make you rich. Having a clear strategy, combined with positive thinking around a possible outcome and the world in general, might.

TAKE A HOLISTIC APPROACH TO LIFE

At the core of what I do is helping people realise the paramount importance of having a holistic approach to life in order to be really, really happy.

During the first, discovery session I ask my clients to score themselves out of 20 on different areas; as we go through their scores together, I show them how all these areas are interlinked.

I've run hundreds of discovery sessions, both one-to-one and in groups, and nine out of 10 times the score on 'General Happiness' will be almost exactly the average score of all the other areas. I find that low scores on one or all of 'Love Life', 'Career' or 'Self-confidence' have the biggest effect on our happiness level, but whether it's 'Fitness', 'Motivation' or 'Self-discipline', they all add up as everything either helps or hurts.

Doing well or even exceeding in some areas while neglecting others will very rarely allow you to be truly happy.

The key to happiness is balance and this is the very best tip I can give you, friends.

ABOUT THE AUTHOR

Michael Serwa is a London based transformation coach. He doesn't improve his clients' lives, he transforms them. He takes them from good to great, using his signature no bullshit approach.

He shows them what they cannot see and he says to them what no one else would dare to say.

Michael has always been passionate about psychology and self-development. In his mid-twenties, he transformed his own life by applying what he'd learnt. Then he took these skills and has since used them to successfully help hundreds of men and women on a one-to-one basis. He's worked with individuals aged from 21 to 65. He's worked with CEOs of multi-billion pound corporations, entrepreneurs, doctors, lawyers, actors, senior executives, teachers, designers, architects, creative and resourceful students.

He also teaches, empowers and inspires people through talks, workshops and seminars. He has spoken at over 200 events on a wide variety of personal development topics.

Visit Michael's website at www.michaelserwa.com, connect with him through social media, or just give him a ring on 07738173913 and have a chat.